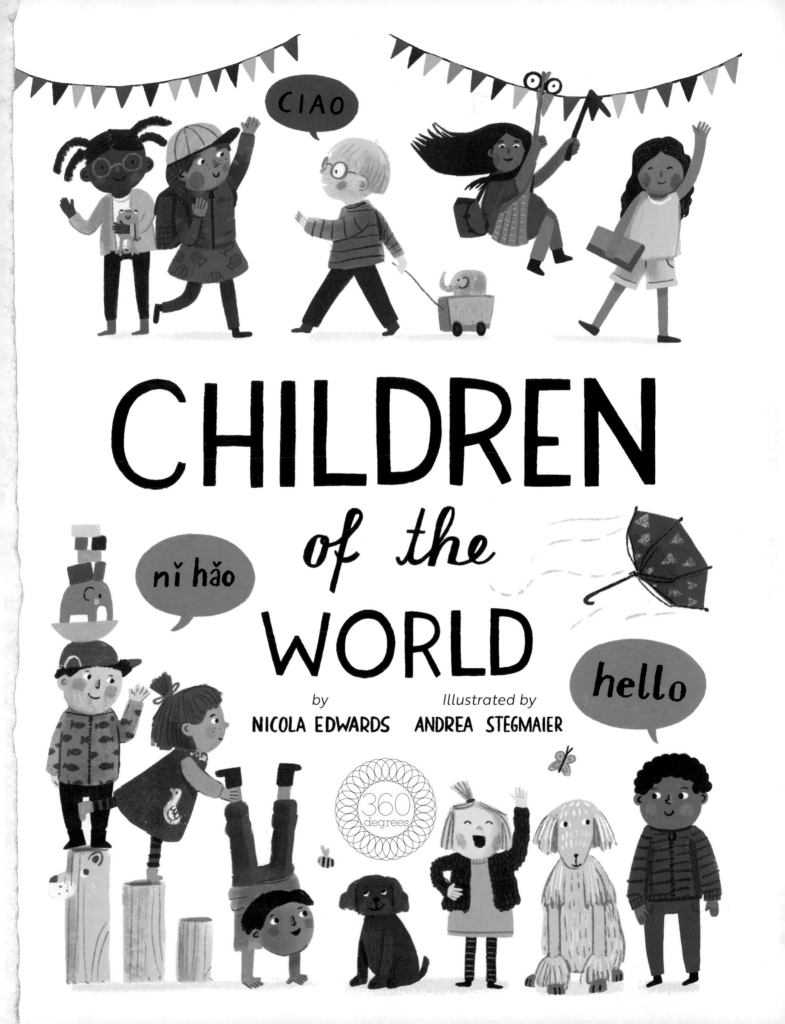

CHILDREN
of the
WORLD

by
NICOLA EDWARDS

illustrated by
ANDREA STEGMAIER

For Ruby and Romy,
welcome to the world
~ N E

For every curious child
~ A S

360 DEGREES, an imprint of Tiger Tales
5 River Road, Suite 128, Wilton, CT 06897
Published in the United States 2022
Originally published in Great Britain 2022
by Caterpillar Books Ltd.
Text by Nicola Edwards
Text copyright © 2022 Caterpillar Books Ltd.
Illustrations copyright © 2022 Andrea Stegmaier
ISBN-13: 978-1-944530-40-2
ISBN-10: 1-944530-40-1
Printed in China
CPB/2800/2041/1121
10 9 8 7 6 5 4 3 2 1

www.tigertalesbooks.com

FSC
www.fsc.org
MIX
Paper from
responsible sources
FSC® C017606

The Forest Stewardship Council® (FSC®) is an international,
non-governmental organization dedicated to promoting
responsible management of the world's forests. FSC®
operates a system of forest certification and product
labeling that allows consumers to identify wood
and wood-based products from well-managed
forests and other controlled sources.

For more information about the FSC®,
please visit their website at www.fsc.org

CHILDREN
of the
WORLD

by
NICOLA EDWARDS

Illustrated by
ANDREA STEGMAIER

360 degrees

CONTENTS

38 CHILDREN IN THEIR WORLD

WELCOME!

The world we live in is vast and magical. Its countries are separated by seas, crisscrossed with mountains, forests, and deserts, and studded with cities, towns, and villages.

The way we live can seem very different depending on where in the world we are. What grows on our trees, the type of weather we have, and what our landscape looks like will make a difference in what we eat, what we wear, and how we travel, play, and celebrate. This variety is what makes the world such a rich and fascinating place to explore.

Our planet is always changing, with global travel and technology keeping us more connected than ever before. This allows us to learn from each other, share the best of different cultures, and see our own lives through fresh eyes.

Whatever our differences may be, there are many things we have in common. We all want to play, to connect with other people, to learn new things.

We're all part of a wider world that we share with plants and animals, and we all have a part to play in deciding what the future of our world will be. When our planet faces something big like climate change or a global pandemic, it reminds us that we're all part of one Earth, and when we come together, we are stronger.

So let's celebrate this incredible world of ours with its skyscrapers and longhouses, huts and houseboats. Whether you keep cats or crickets as pets, eat bao or baguettes, your life is amazing! You are a unique piece of the puzzle that is life on planet Earth.

Now, let's explore the rest of its magic together!

CHILDREN AT HOME

HELLO, CHILDREN OF THE WORLD!

SWAHILI — habari (**ha-BAHR-ee**)

TURKISH — merhaba (**MEHR-hah-bah**)

ALBANIAN — tungjatjeta (**toon-jah-TYEH-tah**)

MANDARIN CHINESE — nǐ hǎo / 你好 (**nee HAO**)

FINNISH — hyvää päivää (**HUU-vaa PIGH-vaa**)

ITALIAN — ciao (**chow**)

RUSSIAN — zdravstvuyte / здравствуйте (**ZDRA-stvooy-tyeh**)

KOREAN — an nyeong ha se yo / 안녕하세요 (**ahn nyeong ha se yo**)

NAVAJO — yá'át'ééh (**yah at eh**)

ARMENIAN — barev dzez / բարև ձեզ (**bah-rev d-zez**)

AMERICAN SIGN LANGUAGE — wave your hand

SPANISH — hola (**oh-lah**)

TAHITIAN — ia orana (**yo-ra-nah**)

KHMER — chum reap suor / ជំរាបសួរ (**chum reap suor**)

MONGOLIAN GERS are round, portable homes with one door, no windows, and no walls inside. Families cook, heat, and cool their home using a stove with a central chimney.

In GRANADA, SPAIN, many people live in CAVES. Some are very basic, while others are luxurious. The caves are cool in the hot, dry climate.

WHAT DOES HOME LOOK LIKE AROUND THE WORLD?

In SYRIA, you will find families living in houses that are built around a CENTRAL COURTYARD. These allow people to enjoy the outdoors but keep their privacy.

HANOKS are traditional KOREAN houses. Their floors can be heated by smoke, and they are supposed to be built with a river in front and a mountain behind them.

The EDE people of VIETNAM live in communal LONGHOUSES on stilts.

HOLLAND is famous for its canals, especially in Amsterdam, its capital city. Thousands of people live on HOUSEBOATS that float on the waters.

In SOUTH AFRICA and ZIMBABWE, you can find the homes of the NDEBELE people painted with bright patterns.

These can be very elongated — around 300 feet (91 m) long!

HONG KONG is sometimes called "the vertical city" as it is packed with SKYSCRAPERS. Many people here have their homes high in the air.

WHAT DOES YOUR KITCHEN LOOK LIKE?

In **MEXICAN** kitchens you may find a traditional wood-burning stove and a fryer as well as a fridge-freezer and gas stove. Many Mexicans like to host big dinners for family and friends. When offering food around the table, all dishes should be passed to the left.

The host sits at the head of the table with the most important guest on his or her right.

Around 90% of **JAPANESE** people live in cities and homes can be quite cramped. A family of four will often live in a home with five rooms, and a Japanese kitchen might not have an oven. Most hot Japanese food is cooked on a stove.

In **SOUTH SUDAN**, electricity is not reliable, so a kitchen might be a fridge and freezer with a stove hooked up to a gas bottle. Here, two meals per day are the norm. Children regularly eat from the same bowl, and men and women will often eat separately.

WHAT'S THAT FOR?

TAGINE, MOROCCO
This specially shaped pot cooks traditional stews (known as "tagines") and also keeps them warm on the table.

AEBLESKIVER PAN, DENMARK
This cast-iron pan makes aebleskiver, a classic Danish dessert of pancake balls filled with jam or applesauce.

LA CHAMBA POTS, COLOMBIA
These clay pots can be used in the oven or on the stove. They make delicious beans — moist, rich, and smoky.

MASALA DABBA, INDIA
This metal tin with its small pots and spoon keeps everyday spices in cooking reach.

WE ARE FAMILY

MOTHER and FATHER

NEPALI (āmā/आमा and bubā/बुबा)

CZECH (matka and otec)

SPANISH (madre and padre)

DANISH (mor and far)

SUDANESE (ibu and bapana)

BROTHER and SISTER

MONGOLIAN (akh/ax and egch/эгч)

PUNJABI (bharā/ਭਰਾ and bhaiṇa/ਭੈਣ)

DID YOU KNOW?

75% of **RUSSIAN** families live in small flats in cities. Some families also have a "dacha," which is like a country cottage.

DID YOU KNOW?

Most **ETHIOPIAN** families live in rural areas. Different branches of the same family will often live clustered around a shared farm. Ethiopian children don't share a surname with their parents. Instead, they take their father's first name as their last name. What would your Ethiopian name be?

GRANDMOTHER and GRANDFATHER

ARABIC (jadda/جَدّة and jadd/جَدّ)

CROATIAN (baka and djed)

GREEK (yia-yia/γιαγιά and pappoús/παππούς)

NORWEGIAN (bestemor and bestefar)

SOMALI (ayeeyo and awoowe)

DID YOU KNOW?
In CAMBODIA, your family name is spoken and written first, followed by your individual name.

DID YOU KNOW?
In NIGERIA, the older you are, the more respect you get from those around you. If you are the oldest child in an Igbo household, you might be called "Senior Brother/Sister," instead of your name.

JAPANESE breakfasts are savory. They include things such as fish, miso soup, pickled vegetables, seaweed, rice, and sticky soybeans.

ICELANDERS might start the day with a thick oatmeal called *hafragrautur*, which can be topped with nuts, raisins, or *skyr* (a yogurt-like cheese).

In **TUNISIA**, *shakshuka* (eggs poached in a rich tomato sauce) is a popular breakfast.

GOOD MORNING! WOULD YOU LIKE SOME BREAKFAST?

JAMAICANS might enjoy a scramble of *ackee* (the national fruit) and saltfish with tomatoes, garlic, chili peppers, and onion. It is sweet, salty, and spicy!

The **LEBANESE** eat *manakish* for breakfast. This spiced flatbread is similar to pizza and can be topped with mince, cheese, or tomatoes.

The **TAIWANESE** enjoy soy milk with their chewy spring onion pancakes and dough fritters.

Nihari is a **PAKISTANI** breakfast dish of spicy meat curry and *naan* (a round, flat bread).

ENGLAND'S traditional breakfast can include eggs, bacon, sausages, toast, baked beans, fried tomatoes, mushrooms, hash browns, and more!

Sfogliatelle, a crunchy, layered pastry with a sweet cheese filling, is enjoyed at breakfast time by **ITALIANS**, especially in Naples.

Many **AMERICANS** eat thick pancakes with maple syrup, bacon, and blueberries for breakfast.

AUSTRALIANS enjoy avocado on toast for breakfast, sometimes topped with an egg.

Bolo de fuba is a **BRAZILIAN** breakfast cake made with cornmeal that often has cheese or shredded coconut in it.

In **MOROCCO**, you might have *beghrir* or "thousand-hole pancakes." Their many holes soak up whatever sauce they are served with.

ETHIOPIANS eat a savory porridge called *genfo* at breakfast. It is formed into a ring with spiced butter in the middle and yogurt alongside it.

Kahvalti is a **TURKISH** breakfast including tomatoes, cucumbers, olives, cheese, sausage, honey, and bread. Something for everyone!

BREAD

HOW THIS STAPLE VARIES ACROSS THE GLOBE

BAO — These soft, pillowy, steamed **TAIWANESE** buns can have various fillings. The pork and spring onion mix is a popular option.

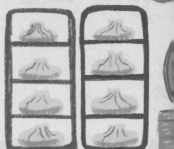

COTTAGE LOAF
This traditional **ENGLISH** bread is made from a smaller ball of dough on top of a bigger ball.

BAGUETTE — This long, thin loaf is a **FRENCH** icon.

PÃO DE QUEIJO
These puffy, round buns from **BRAZIL** are made using cheese and tapioca flour.

BAMMY — This fried **JAMAICAN** flatbread is made from cassava root.

RĒWENA PARĀOA
A traditional **MAORI** sourdough potato bread from **NEW ZEALAND**.

PAN DE MUERTO — This sweet bread is served for **MEXICO**'s Day of the Dead celebrations. It smells like aniseed and is often glazed with orange juice or topped with colored sugar.

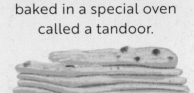

NAAN — This famous, savory **INDIAN** flatbread is baked in a special oven called a tandoor.

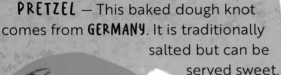

PRETZEL — This baked dough knot comes from **GERMANY**. It is traditionally salted but can be served sweet.

HEMBESHA — A round, cardamom-spiced flatbread eaten in **ERITREA** at celebrations.

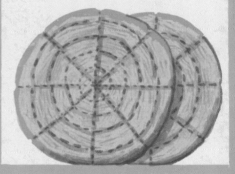

BARMBRACK — This sweet **IRISH** tea bread, studded with raisins and sultanas, is often toasted and buttered.

CHALLAH — This braided **ISRAELI** loaf is often made for Shabbat (the Jewish day of rest).

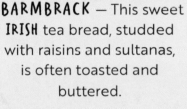

BUBLIK — A ring-shaped dough roll from **UKRAINE** that is generally denser and chewier than a bagel.

CIABATTA — A classic **ITALIAN** bread. Its name means "slipper" because of its shape.

KULICH — This tall, cake-like sweet bread is a **RUSSIAN** Easter tradition. It is often eaten with *paskha*, a kind of cheesecake.

UNIQUE WORLD FOOD

The **PERUVIAN** fruit **LUCUMA** is generally not eaten fresh because it has a texture similar to dried egg yolk, but its sweet taste makes it popular as a flavoring in other things like smoothies and desserts.

The **BRAZILIAN** condiment **FAROFA** is a toasted cassava flour that is sprinkled on all kinds of things, like meat, fruit, vegetables, or the national stew, *feijoada*.

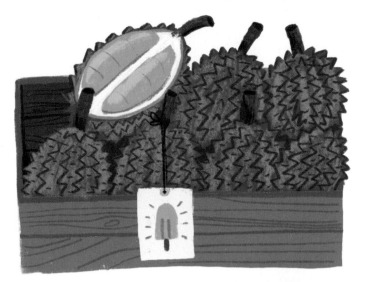

The **MUSANG KING DURIAN** is a **MALAYSIAN** fruit well known for its stinky fragrance, which has been compared to ripe cheese or even rotting meat. Despite the smell, the fruit's flesh is sweet and custardy.

PAP is a kind of maize that is very popular in **SOUTH AFRICA**. It is made into noodles, porridge with milk and sugar, or even a stew with meat and gravy.

The **FEIJOA** fruit is a national treasure in **NEW ZEALAND**. Its taste is complicated, with hints of mint, pineapple, and apple, and it is popular in smoothies and as a raw snack.

RUSSIANS eat the "Mockba," which is a combination of tuna, sardines, salmon, mackerel, herring, and onions.

In INDIA, you might see pizza featuring pickled ginger, mince, and paneer cheese.

HOWEVER YOU SLICE IT, WE ALL LOVE PIZZA!

BRAZILIANS are open-minded about toppings. You might find peas, corn, raisins, and hard-boiled eggs on a slice here.

Mayo jaga is a mix of mayonnaise, potato, corn, onion, and bacon used on JAPANESE pizzas.

In SWEDEN, peanut, chicken, banana, pineapple, and curry powder-topped pizza is popular!

Pepperoni is the most ordered pizza topping in the UNITED STATES.

The **PORTUGUESE** enjoy onions and *linguica* (a garlicky sausage) on their pizzas.

In **HOLLAND**, shawarma (kebab meat) is a popular pizza topping.

Tarte flambée is a traditional **FRENCH** pizza-style dish that uses bacon, onion, and cream.

PAKISTAN enjoys pizza with *achari* chicken, which is chicken marinated in yogurt and *achari* pickling spice.

In **AUSTRALIA**, pizza can be an all-day-breakfast affair with ham, bacon, and egg.

COSTA RICANS enjoy prawns and shredded coconut on pizza.

NATIONAL DISHES FROM AROUND THE WORLD

POUTINE

CANADA
These french fries are covered in cheese curd and a tangy chicken or turkey gravy. Pour the gravy just before serving to avoid soggy fries!

COU-COU and FLYING FISH

BARBADOS
Cou-cou is an okra and cornmeal porridge. The flying fish it is served with might be steamed with spices and lime juice or fried.

GOULASH

HUNGARY
This spicy meat and vegetable stew has a tomato and paprika sauce.

CEVICHE

PERU
Here, chunks of raw fish are marinated with lime juice and served with onions, chili peppers, and garlic.

GREECE
In moussaka, lamb mince, fried eggplant and potatoes are layered under a white sauce and baked.

MOUSSAKA

PASTEL DE CHOCLO

CHILE
This casserole is filled with beef, onions, raisins, and olives, with a corn crust.

BRAZIL
This stew of beef, pork, and beans is generally served with rice, greens, and sliced oranges.

FEIJOADA

ENGLAND
This meal consists of roasted meat with gravy, boiled vegetables, and roast potatoes.

ROAST DINNER

KOREA
Here, sliced beef is marinated then grilled. You might see it wrapped in lettuce or spinach, with *kimchi* (pickled cabbage) on the side.

BEEF BULGOGI

RAMEN

JAPAN
This is a noodle broth with sliced pork, seaweed, mushrooms, bean sprouts, and a boiled egg in it.

GEORGIA
This bread is baked with a cheese filling, then topped with butter and an egg.

KHACHAPURI

SOUTH AFRICA
Curried mince is topped with a kind of egg custard in this dish. It is often served with rice and chutney.

SUCCOTASH

BOBOTIE

EQUATORIAL GUINEA
This dish includes corn, butter beans, peppers, tomatoes, and other fried vegetables.

INDONESIA
This stir-fried rice includes prawns, shallots, and soy sauce and has a fried egg on top.

NASI GORENG

HOW ARE YOU FEELING TODAY?

HAPPY

GERMAN — glücklich (**gloo-cleekh**)

ARABIC — alsaeida / السعيدة
(**ES-igh-ee-duh**)

DANISH — glad (**glad**)

JAPANESE — ureshii / うれしい
(**ooh-ress-hee**)

SWAHILI — furaha (**foo-ra-ha**)

INDONESIAN — gembira (**gem-BEE-rah**)

SAD

DUTCH — verdrietig (**fur-DREE-tukh**)

SPANISH — triste (**TREE-stay**)

KOREAN — seulpeoyo / 슬퍼요 (**sul-poy-yo**)

POLISH — smutny (**smoot-neh**)

HINDI — udaas / उदास
(**oo-DUS**)

GREEK — lypiménos / λυπημένος
(**li-pee-MEN-os**)

ANGRY

ITALIAN — arrabbiato (**ah-ra-bee-AH-toh**)

CZECH — rozzlobený (**roz-LOH-beh-nee**)

MANDARIN CHINESE — shēngqì / 生气
(**shung-TSCHEE**)

TURKISH — kızgın (**kuz-gun**)

NORWEGIAN — sint (**sint**)

RUSSIAN — serdityj / сердитый
(**seer-DEE-teey**)

SURPRISED

FRENCH — étonnée (**eh-toh-NAY**)

THAI — Praħlād cı / ประหลาดใจ
(**pra-laht JAI**)

PORTUGUESE — surpreso (**soor-PRAY-zo**)

DUTCH — verrast (**fir-UST**)

FINNISH — yllättynyt
(**OOH-lat-en-oot**)

WELSH — synnu (**SUN-ni**)

IT'S RAINING CATS AND DOGS!

On a visit to **RUSSIA**'s State Hermitage Museum, you might be surprised to find around 70 **CATS** on patrol! Cats have been in residence since 1745, when the original palace was in need of mouse control!

In **CHINA**, singing **CRICKETS** are thought to be lucky. Children often keep them in decorative cages as pets. They might even hold cricket-singing competitions.

In **JAPAN**, horned **BEETLES** are considered collectable pets.

Their miniature size means they're ideal in small Japanese apartments. The rhino beetle is known as "kabutomushi" in Japanese, which literally means "samurai helmet bug."

The **UNITED STATES** has the most pet **DOGS** in the world, and they are treated as part of the family. But not every culture treats animals as pets. Most **MONGOLIAN** families have dogs, but they are thought of as working animals.

Globally, **BRAZIL** has the most small dogs per person.

Meanwhile, **SAUDI ARABIA** has the most large-breed dogs.

In **PERU**, **ALPACAS** are popular pets.

In the **UNITED STATES**, a good dog is a friendly companion.

They have silky fur that can be shorn and sold to add to a family's income. Alpacas have a loyal nature and can respond to simple commands.

In **UGANDA**, a good dog protects a family's property and keeps thieves away!

COUGHS AND COLDS AND HOW WE CURE THEM

HOLLAND
Salty "salmiak licorice" is used to make a soothing throat candy with a taste that takes some getting used to!

IRAN
Here, you might eat a plate of mashed, cooked turnips to combat a cold.

JAPAN
Umeboshi, or sour pickled plum, is eaten or made into a tea with lemon and ginger to prevent and cure colds, flus, and other illnesses.

INDIA
Cure your sore throat with turmeric-laced "golden milk."

CHINA
Forget chicken soup. Try some dried lizard soup, which also contains yams and dates, to help with a sore throat or cold.

DOMINICAN REPUBLIC
For a sore-throat cure, cut two passionfruit and one onion in half, boil them in water, and add honey.

RUSSIA
Gogol mogol, a hot drink with egg yolk, honey, and water, is a popular cure for colds here. Garlic is also used, and during flu season, some children even keep cloves of garlic in their pockets to ward off illness!

IT'S TIME FOR BED!

WHERE DO WE SLEEP?

The **CHARPAI** or **MANJI** is a traditional **INDIAN** bed that has a wooden frame with a woven top made from cotton, date leaves, or other natural materials. It keeps sleepers cool in warm weather.

The **CHINESE KANG BED** is a large brick platform with an oven built underneath it. Whole families can sleep together on the platform, and the surface can also be used during the day for socializing and staying warm.

In **KENYA** and many other **AFRICAN** cultures, **SLINGS** are used to carry sleeping babies, leaving parents free to go about their day. Kenyans often use a bright, printed cloth called a *kanga* to wrap the baby in.

In **AFGHANISTAN**, it's unusual to have a special bedroom for sleeping in. Mattresses and blankets are generally laid out in a living room at night and put aside during the day. Families tend to sleep in the same room.

In MOZAMBIQUE, NETTED BEDS are common to keep sleepers safe from malaria-carrying mosquitoes.

Traditional FUTON beds can be rolled up during the day.

They are popular in JAPAN as they help save space in small homes.

Some VENEZUELAN HIWI people sleep in HAMMOCKS woven from moriche palm leaves. They don't use pillows or blankets.

HOW AND WHEN DO WE SLEEP?

The hunter-gatherer EFE people of ZAIRE sleep when they feel tired, whether it's day or night.

In SPAIN, it is traditional to have a lunchtime nap or rest, called a siesta, each day.

Kids in HOLLAND often go to bed as early as 6:30 pm, while in ARGENTINA, it's normal for children to be up until 10 pm.

SCANDINAVIAN infants commonly nap outside in cold weather — parents believe fresh air is healthy.

GOOD NIGHT!

MANDARIN CHINESE — wǎn'ān/晚安 (**WAN-an**)

RUSSIAN — spokoynoy nochi / спокойной ночи (**spok-OY-noy NO-chi**)

ITALIAN — buona notte (**BWON-a NOT-ay**)

SWEDISH — godnatt (**go-NAT**)

FINNISH — hyvää yötä (**HOO-vah OOH-er-ta**)

SWAHILI — usiku mwema (**ooh-see-koo mweh-ma**)

SPANISH — buenas noches (**bwen-as no-chez**)

GREEK — kalinikta / καληνύχτα (**kah-lee-NIKT-ah**)

ARABIC — tisbah ala khair / تصبح على خير (**tuss-bah el-la kher**)

HINDI — shubh raatri / शुभ रात्रि (**shub raa-tree**)

GERMAN — gute Nacht (**GOO-teh naakt**)

FRENCH — bonne nuit (**bon nwee**)

37

CHILDREN IN THEIR WORLD

WHAT'S THE WEATHER LIKE WHERE YOU ARE?

In the INDIAN village of MAWSYNRAM, in the state of MEGHALAYA, it is so rainy that villagers try to dull the sound by lining their homes with grass. Locals can be seen using woven "knup" umbrellas that are worn like turtle shells!

LA RINCONADA, PERU, has an altitude of more than 16,700 feet (5,090 m). Half of the Earth's atmosphere sits below it!

You'd have to hold on to your hat if you wanted to move to WELLINGTON, NEW ZEALAND, where winds can get as high as 154 miles per hour (248 kph)! During the windiest year on record, the city experienced gale-force winds on 233 out of 365 days.

Are you attached to having a roof over your head? Well, ASWAN in southern EGYPT has so little rainfall (less than a quarter of an inch a year!) that some residents don't bother with roofs and enjoy a clear view of the stars from their beds.

What's life like in the middle of a volcano?

The JAPANESE volcanic island, AOGASHIMA, is remote, quiet, and surprisingly green, with a tiny elementary school for around 25 students. The volcano hasn't erupted for more than 200 years but is still classified as active, so residents take their chances living here!

OYMYAKON, in SIBERIAN RUSSIA, has been known to get as cold as -96°F (-71°C). Mobile phones can't function here due to the temperature, and you can't wear glasses outside as they would quickly freeze to your face!

Summers in COOBER PEDY in AUSTRALIA last around six months, and temperatures often rise to 104°F (40°C), so many people choose to live in underground houses called "dugouts."

HOW WE TRAVEL

Ice Angels are ice boats in **WISCONSIN** in the **UNITED STATES** that have air propellers so they can glide over the ice when it is too thin to drive over, but too frozen for regular ferries.

VENICE, ITALY, has a huge network of canals. While most of the gondolas (rowing boats) are for tourist travel, the *gondola da traghetto* ferries locals across the city's Grand Canal.

In **LA PAZ, BOLIVIA**'s capital, you can use the solar-powered Teleférico (cable car) to travel to nearby **EL ALTO**. Travelers get amazing bird's-eye views over the world's highest city.

HAVANA in **CUBA** has black "cocotaxis," shaped like coconuts, to take locals around. There is also a yellow cocotaxi for tourist travel.

Tuk tuks are three-wheeled motor-rickshaws popular across **SOUTHEAST ASIA**, but especially in the **THAI** capital, **BANGKOK**. The name comes from the sputtering noise made by early models.

In **NAIROBI, KENYA**, you can pick up a ride in a *matatu*. These small, flashy buses compete for the most colorful lights and the best Kenyan music and graffiti design.

The Maglev (magnetic levitation) train in **SHANGHAI, CHINA**, is lightning-fast and uses repelling magnets to hover a few inches above the tracks.

The **GERMAN** Schwebebahn is a monorail with cars that hang from the track like a carnival ride! Thousands of passengers use it daily to travel through Wuppertal.

In parts of the **PHILIPPINES**, the *habal-habal* is a popular way to travel. The most complicated type of this adapted motorcycle can seat 13 people plus luggage, balancing on wooden planks!

The *nori* or bamboo train of **CAMBODIA** carries around 15 people on a double-bed-sized bamboo platform. It is known for being cheap and bumpy!

MEETING AND GREETING

In the **PHILIPPINES**, if you're greeting someone older than you, press your forehead against the other person's knuckles and say,

"MANA PO,"

which means "Your hands, please."

In **BOTSWANA**, put out your right arm, put your left hand on your right elbow, and take the other person's hand, then lace your thumbs together, before returning to the regular hand-shaking position and saying:

"LAE KAE?"

or "How are you?" in Setswana.

INVENT A SECRET HANDSHAKE WITH YOUR FRIENDS

In **MALAYSIA**, if you reach out your hands to touch fingertips with another person and then put your hand on your heart, you are showing that your greeting is heartfelt.

In **NEW ZEALAND**, you may be greeted with a "hongi" by a Māori person. This special greeting is all about the sharing of breath and involves pressing both your nose and forehead against the other person.

"HONGI"

In **UKRAINE**, three kisses are used as a greeting. You start on the left cheek and then go right and left again.

In **JAPAN**, children learn early on how to properly greet people with a bow. The lower you bow, the more respect you are showing the other person.

DOES YOUR FAMILY HAVE A SPECIAL GREETING?

GREENLANDERS have a greeting for close friends and family called a "kunik" where you press your nose and upper lip against the other person and breathe on them.

HOW DO YOU SAY PLEASE AND THANK YOU AROUND THE WORLD?

PLEASE

HEBREW — bevekshah / בבקשה (be-va-ka-sha)

SAMOAN — fa'amolemole (fah-ah-molay-molay)

RUSSIAN — pozhaluista / пожалуйста (pa-ZHAL-sta)

BALINESE — suksma (suks-maa)

PORTUGUESE — por favor (por fah-VOR)

SLOVENIAN — prosim (PROH-seem)

PERSIAN — lotfan / لطف (lut-fan)

AFRIKAANS — asseblief (a-seh-bleef)

SWEDISH — snälla du (SNAH-la durh)

THANK YOU

JAPANESE — arigatô / ありがとう (ah-ree-GAH-toh)

HAWAIIAN — mahalo (ma-HA-lo)

ICELANDIC — takk (tahk)

ROMANIAN — mulţumesc (mool-tzoo-MESK)

BENGALI — dhonnobad / ধন্যবাদ (dhon-no-baad)

GREEK — efharisto / ευχαριστώ (ef-hah-rees-TOH)

GERMAN — danke (DUN-kuh)

VIETNAMESE — cảm ơn (gaam urn)

FRENCH — merci (mair-SEE)

CHILDREN AT SCHOOL

Until 2017, **PHUMACHANGTANG, TIBET,** had the highest elementary school in the world. At 16,480 feet (5,022 m), it was almost as high as Mount Everest's base camp! This remote site is currently closed, but there are plans to reopen it as a preschool.

Most **GERMAN** schoolchildren don't wear a uniform, so they can express themselves through their clothes, but Kindergarten Wolfartsweier takes being unique to a new level. Designed to look like a white cat, children enter the building through its mouth and can exit by sliding down the cat's tail!

All **DUTCH** students start school on their 4th birthday, so there are new kids joining class all year.

FINNISH children start school at seven years old.

Because floods are so common in **BANGLADESH,** around 100 floating schools with solar-powered internet access have been built on boats.

At **FRENCH** elementary schools, it's common for fresh bread to be delivered every morning for lunch. Food is eaten on china plates with silver cutlery, and lunch can last up to two hours.

In **LOS PINOS, COLOMBIA**, children travel to school on a zip line through the rain forest!

In **SOUTH KOREA**, public schools do not have cleaning crews. Students mop and sweep their school themselves!

Because most of **ETHIOPIA** is rural, many children have to walk several miles each way to get to school.

INDIA's City Montessori School in **LUCKNOW** has the most students of any school in the world — more than 56,000! **INDIA** also has a Train Platform School. It allows poor and homeless children to gather around train stations and learn everything from reading and writing to puppetry.

In **SAN PABLO**, in the **PHILIPPINES**, a school created from plastic bottles has made treasure out of trash. The bottles have been filled with mud to become three times stronger than concrete!

THE WORLD OF WORDS

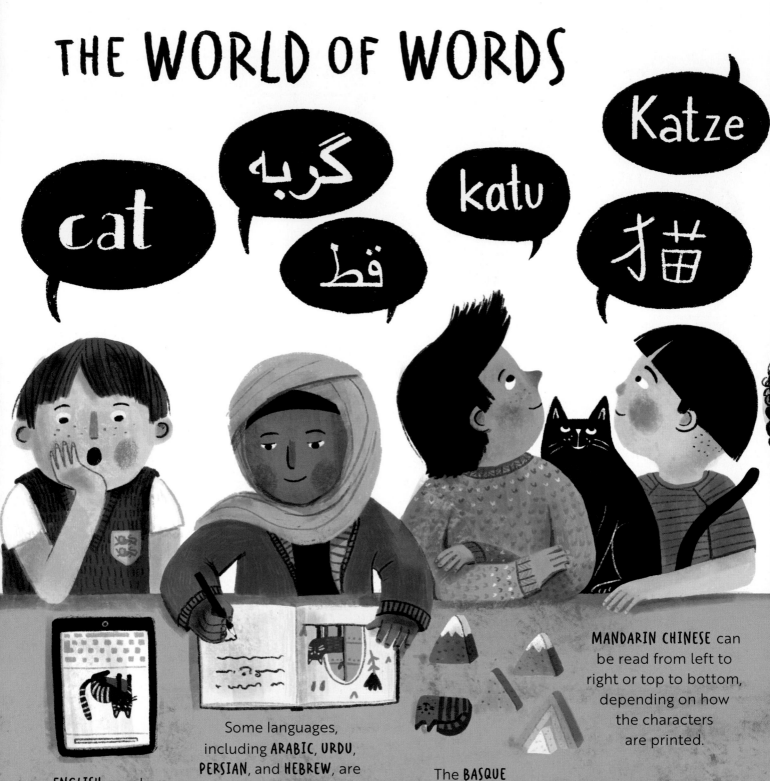

cat

گربه

قط

katu

Katze

猫

ENGLISH speakers may be surprised to know that 95% of spoken languages are not in use on the internet.

Some languages, including **ARABIC**, **URDU**, **PERSIAN**, and **HEBREW**, are written from right to left.

The **BASQUE** language is spoken in the Pyrenees mountains between France and Spain, but it isn't linked to French, Spanish, or any other living language. Its origins are a mystery!

MANDARIN CHINESE can be read from left to right or top to bottom, depending on how the characters are printed.

ikati

pusi

ネコ

Although the **UNITED STATES** and **BRITAIN** both speak **ENGLISH**, they use two separate sign languages — ASL and BSL — which can't be understood by the speakers of the other language.

There are 11 official languages in **SOUTH AFRICA.**

JAPANESE has three different kinds of writing: *hiragana, kanji,* and *katakana. Katakana* is used to spell out words that originally came from other cultures.

In **PAPUA NEW GUINEA**, 840 different languages are spoken. The country is covered with thick rain forest, so many groups have stayed separate, and their languages haven't mixed over time.

Try writing your name in *katakana* using this alphabet key!

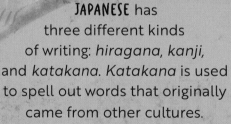

ワ wa	ラ ra	ヤ ya	マ ma	ハ ha	ナ na	タ ta	サ sa	カ ka	ア a
	リ ri		ミ mi	ヒ hi	ニ ni	チ chi	シ shi	キ ki	イ i
	ル ru	ユ yu	ム mu	フ fu/hu	ヌ nu	ツ tsu	ス su	ク ku	ウ u
ン n	レ re		メ me	ヘ he	ネ ne	テ te	セ se	ケ ke	エ e
ヲ wo	ロ ro	ヨ yo	モ mo	ホ ho	ノ no	ト to	ソ so	コ ko	オ o

IT'S TIME TO PLAY!
WORLD GAMES

Hopscotch, a game where players hop and jump over squares drawn on the ground, is popular around the world. In **FRANCE**, the game is played on a giant snail.

Children in **ZIMBABWE** play *kudoda*. Players sit around a ring filled with stones. You must throw one stone in the air and then pick up as many others from the ring as you can before catching the stone you threw.

In a **CHINESE** game called "catch the dragon's tail," the child at the front of the line is the dragon's head, and the child at the back is the tail. The head must catch the tail!

ISRAELI children use apricot stones (or *go-gos*) to play *go-go-im*. Different-sized holes are cut into a shoebox and given a value based on how difficult it is to throw in a go-go.

"Rock, paper, scissors," played using hand gestures, is famous the world over.

Scissors cut paper, paper covers rock, and rock dulls scissors.

In **INDONESIA**, the game is *semut*, *orang*, *gajah* (ant, human, elephant).

WORLD TOYS

The aim of the **JAPANESE** game *daruma otoshi* is to knock the central blocks of the tower out without making the daruma on top fall over.

KENYAN children use scrap materials like sticks, wire, and cornstalks to make their own toy vehicles, called *galimoto*.

The Rubik's cube was invented in **HUNGARY** in 1974. It is the most popular puzzle toy in the world!

DOLLS HAVE ALWAYS BEEN POPULAR, BUT HOW DO THEY VARY FROM PLACE TO PLACE?

INUIT dolls are made from soapstone and bone and dressed in fur.

Beaded dolls are made by the **ZULU** community. Patterns in the beadwork represent different messages.

Corn husk dolls are traditionally made by **NATIVE AMERICAN SENECA** people.

Bisque porcelain dolls were made in 19th-century **EUROPE**. They had realistic-looking skin and hair.

RUSSIAN *matryoshka* dolls are hollow with layers of smaller and smaller dolls inside.

EXPRESS YOURSELF!

ITALIAN — allora! (ah-lor-ah) = **come on!**

SPANISH — guau! (gw-ow) = **wow!**

TAGALOG — gigil! (gi-gil) = **oh, how cute!**

GERMAN — igitt! (ig-git) = **yuck!**

PORTUGUESE — ótimo! (oh-chee-moh) = **great!**

GREEK — youpee! / Γιούπι! (yo-pee) = **yay!**

JAPANESE — yatta! / やった! (ya-TA) = **I did it!**

FRENCH — n'importe quoi! (nam-porte kwuh) = **nonsense!**

SWEDISH — vad häftigt! (vaad hef-tit) = **how cool!**

BENGALI — ki dāruna! / কি দারুন (ki dah-ROON) = **wow!**

POLISH — bo tak! (boh tak) = **because I said so!**

TURKISH — çabuk ol! (ch-book ohl) = **hurry up!**

NORWEGIAN — det er ikke sant! (day uh reek-ke sunt)
= **that can't be true!**

LITHUANIAN — valio! (vah-lee-oh) = **hooray!**

TAMIL — aiyoh! / ஐயோ·ஈஹ் (ee-yo) = **oh, no!**

KOREAN — daebak! / 대박 (hay-bukh) = **awesome!**

MIND YOUR MANNERS!

JAPAN — Slurping your noodles and soup means that you're enjoying your food, but passing food using chopsticks is very bad manners.

ETHIOPIA — There is a tradition of hand-feeding friends and family. This act is called *gursha*, and it is meant to encourage trust and bonding.

INDIA — It's rude to waste food here, so try to finish everything on your plate. But only eat with your right hand!

FRANCE — It's not polite to rest your hands in your lap at the dinner table.

Cutting lettuce is also a no-no. You should fold your lettuce leaves around your fork instead.

CHINA — It's impolite to finish all of the food on your plate as it's a sign your host hasn't given you enough. Instead, leave a little bit, and burp loudly to show that you enjoyed your meal.

ISRAEL — It's common to serve *pitzuchim,* or roasted nuts and seeds, after a meal. It is perfectly polite to crack the shells with your teeth and spit them into a container.

56

GHANA — When you enter a room, make sure you greet everyone, even if they are strangers in a train station. If you don't, you may find people keep staring at you as they wait to be greeted.

BULGARIA — Remember that, here, nodding your head means "no," while shaking your head from side to side means "yes"! Confusing!

TURKEY — Here, you shake your head when you want someone to repeat what was said. To say "no," you click your tongue and toss your head back.

VENEZUELA — Showing up early or even on time for a social event is frowned on, especially if there will be food and drink. It is a sign that you are greedy! It's better to arrive about 15 minutes late.

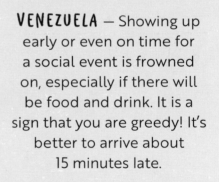

JAPAN — If you hand someone something here, make sure you do it with both hands to show that you are sincere.

SRI LANKA — In the United States, it's friendly to pat a child on the head, but Sri Lankans would see this as extremely rude. For Buddhists, the top of the head is the most spiritual part of the body and shouldn't be messed with.

SUPERSTITIONS AROUND THE WORLD

ARE YOU FEELING LUCKY?

It is bad luck to wrap birthday presents in black-and-white paper in INDIA.

In the UNITED STATES, the number 13 is unlucky, but in ITALY, it is the number 17 you have to watch out for.

16 ~~17~~ 18

In SERBIA, spill some water behind your friend to bring him or her good luck.

Many TURKISH people carry eye-shaped glass amulets or *nazar* to ward off the evil eye, which is thought to cause misfortune.

In ENGLAND, it's considered bad luck to open an umbrella indoors.

Don't whistle around a RUSSIAN house because you will be thought to be whistling all the household's money away.

Stepping in dog poop with your left foot in FRANCE is meant to give you good luck. (It's unlucky if you step in it with your right foot, though.)

Owls are a symbol of bad luck in KENYA.

If you hear thunder in JAPAN, you should quickly cover your belly button so you aren't unlucky enough to have the god of thunder, Raijin, eat it.

In HUNGARY, it's unlucky to sit at the corner of the table.

In INDIA, the elephant is a symbol of good luck, wisdom, and power.

In EGYPT, you'll be scolded for opening and closing scissors without cutting anything. Keeping scissors open is also thought to be unlucky.

Spiders' webs are lucky in UKRAINE, and here they even trim their Christmas trees with decorations that look like dewy spiders' silk.

HOW WE CELEBRATE

In **JAMAICA** you might get "antiqued," or coated in flour, by friends and family on your birthday.

On Easter Saturday in **CORFU**, families smash pots in the streets from their balconies to celebrate the coming of spring. Visitors had better watch where they are walking!

At the Songkran Water Festival in **THAILAND**, the new year is celebrated. Children and adults alike flood the streets with water guns, buckets, water balloons, and hoses, ready to soak anyone they come across.

In **RUSSIA**, it's traditional to hang little presents on a clothesline at a birthday party. Each child there will pull one off as a party favor.

In Bariloche in **ARGENTINA**, an enormous chocolate egg is built in the town square as an Easter centerpiece. Once it's complete, cranes are used to break it into chunks that are distributed to the people.

In the 13 days before Christmas, the Yule Lads visit ICELANDIC children, leaving presents for those who have been good and rotten potatoes for the ones who've been bad. The Yule Lads have nicknames like Spoon-licker, Door-slammer, and Sausage-swiper!

Just before Christmas in San Fernando in the PHILIPPINES, the Giant Lantern Festival is held. The colorful lanterns can be up to 20 feet (6 m) in size.

In November or December each year, JEWISH people celebrate a festival of lights called Hanukkah. Children are given chocolate coins and eat *latkes* (potato pancakes) and doughnuts.

Holi is a Hindu festival celebrated in INDIA. Brightly colored powder is thrown all around in a joyful celebration of the coming of spring.

In VIETNAM, there are no specific birthdays — everyone gets a year older on Tet (New Year's Day). During this festival, Vietnamese people decorate their houses with peach and apricot blooms.

GOOD-BYE, CHILDREN OF THE WORLD!

JAPANESE — sayōnara / さようなら (**sai-OH-nar-ah**)

SLOVENIAN — nasvidenje (**nas-VEE-dan-yeh**)

FRENCH — au revoir (**oh ruh-VWAHR**)

MANDARIN CHINESE — zài jiàn / 再见 (**tzai JIEN**)

ARABIC — ma'a as-salaama / مع السلامة (**MAH seh-lah-mah**)

HEBREW — shalom / שלום (**shah-LOHM**)

TAGALOG — paalam na (**puh-AH-lam nah**)

AMERICAN SIGN LANGUAGE — hold palm facing forward, fold down fingers, and open palm again

HAWAIIAN — aloha (**ah-LOH-ha**)

DANISH — farvel (**fa-VEL**)

AFRIKAANS — totsiens (**TOTE-seens**)

FIJIAN — moce (**moth-ey**)

HINDI — namaste / नमस्ते (**nah-mah-stay**)

HUNGARIAN — viszlát (**vis-LAHT**)

BELARUSIAN - da pabačennia / да пабачэння (**da pa-ba-chen-ya**)

WE ARE ALL CHILDREN OF THE WORLD....

We might **LIVE** in brightly painted houses,

EAT durians with spiky skins,

PLAY with porcelain dolls,

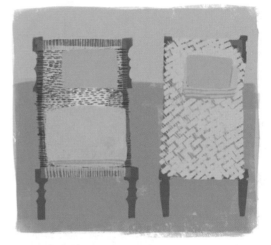

or **SLEEP** in beds with woven tops.

BUT **NO MATTER** WHAT OUR DIFFERENCES ARE, CHILDREN OF THE WORLD STAND TOGETHER!